Bibliographic information published by the German National Library:

The German National Library lists this publication in the National Bibliography; detailed bibliographic data are available on the Internet at http://dnb.dnb.de .

Imprint:

Copyright © 2007 GRIN Verlag, Open Publishing GmbH
Print and binding: Books on Demand GmbH, Norderstedt Germany
ISBN: 9783640477012

This book at GRIN:

http://www.grin.com/en/e-book/138850/a-new-and-historical-theatre-in-bertolt-brecht-s-life-of-galileo

Kristina Kolb

A "new" and "historical" theatre in Bertolt Brecht's "Life of Galileo"?

GRIN Publishing

GRIN - Your knowledge has value

Since its foundation in 1998, GRIN has specialized in publishing academic texts by students, college teachers and other academics as e-book and printed book. The website www.grin.com is an ideal platform for presenting term papers, final papers, scientific essays, dissertations and specialist books.

Visit us on the internet:

http://www.grin.com/

http://www.facebook.com/grincom

http://www.twitter.com/grin_com

A "new" and "historical" theatre in Bertolt Brecht's *Life of Galileo*?

The Almeida Theatre charges around £22 per performance, the National Theatre even more. Most probably these were not the kind of figures that Brecht, a leftwing, if not to say Marxist writer, had in mind when he set out to create a theatre for the masses, to be driven out into "the suburbs". However, just like Brecht's ideas about theatre changed throughout his career as a dramaturg and a playwright, most prominently embodied in the three different versions of *Life of Galileo* (in addition to minor variations of different productions Brecht was involved in himself), moving away from the formalist epic theatre towards a dialectical one, so have our perceptions of the theatre, and what was new and revolutionary during the early years of the play's production has now been reappropriated by *high culture*. While Brecht displayed a great awareness of the need to continuously adapt his play in order to not only make it appropriate for the times, but also to *maintain* it appropriate in the light of *changing times*, different productions of the play have only done so with limited courage and success, leading to the sad result that what *Life of Galileo* once embodied is usually not entirely what it embodies now.

Brecht lived at a time of ideological crisis. During his lifetime he experienced and bore witness to two World Wars, the rise of fascism, political persecution and the exploitation of scientific advance, culminating in the atomic bombings of Hiroshima in 1945. New advances in science changed previously held beliefs about life, and his involvement with Marxism in the 1920s led him to believe that a new society was to arise and that it was his responsibility as an artist to contribute to its formation and to represent it. The inevitable result was his dissatisfaction with the "old" forms of European theatre based on Aristotle, which, in the face of changing contemporary circumstances were, Brecht thought, inadequate to represent social reality.

Brecht's "new" and "historical" theatre was in opn opposition to the European tradition of theatre that, up to that point, had to a large extent been defined in terms of Aristotle's theory of drama. In Aristotelian tragedy the fall of the great (usually caused by wrong decisions) is supposed to cause empathy in the spectator and lead, thus, to Aristotelian catharsis. It usually takes places in only one setting and over a very limited period of time, aiming for a "closed" form of drama with a clear, linear plot and with a definite beginning, main part and end. ". Opposed to Aristotles' "closed" drama, Brecht aimed for an "open" form, thematically reflected in the play by the "shut in" ptolemaic system based on Aristotle's world view. The individual episodes were to be only loosely connected, all contributing,

1

however, to the play's main theme. Instead, the scenes are united by means of the repetition of the main characters, settings and motifs. While Aristotelian theatre aimed at the identification of the spectator with the character and at emotional involvement, Brecht believed that, in order for the audience to be critical and intellectually involved in the play, distance was needed, the audience needed to be *alienated*. His new, epic theatre was not to be "culinary", or, in other words, for easy consumption, but to appeal to reason.

As critics and playwrights claim alike, Brecht revolutionarized the theatre. Through a new form of drama, he wanted to create a theatre for the masses, which was to "use the means of representation to create an understanding of the "rules" by which society was "governed"[1]. This accurate representation of social reality was to serve the aim of entertaining the "children of the scientific age". What Brecht missed in the bourgeois theatre, which he heavily criticized, was fun. "In all the easily heated, prettily lighted, money-devouring, imposing looking theatres, and in all the stuff that is offered in them, there is no longer five cents' worth of *fun*."[2] By providing a pleasurable theatre for the "children of the scientific age", Brecht was simultaneously attempting to unite learning and entertainment, creating pleasure out of the dialectics in life[3], opposing the "high" modernists' emphasis on aesthetics.

Brecht himself wrote three distinct versions of *Life of Galileo* and different translations and interpretations of the play make it impossible to treat it like a single entity. Since the so-called "American version" of the play has formed the basis for most subsequent performances, it is this version I will be referring to when discussing Brecht's own realization of his ideas. However, since the text was written for performance, the play's success, with reference to Brecht's aims, largely depends on the decisions and interpretations of the corresponding directors so that the text cannot be regarded as entirely authoritative. Furthermore, I will, in particular, look at Losey's 1947 production as well as his 1975 film version, both based on Laughton's translation of the play and, thus, show how far Brecht's ideas about theatre were embodied in *Life of Galileo*, as written by Brecht himself (with Laughton's collaboration), as well as through two somewhat differenttypes of representation (theatre and film) at different times.

As Brecht elaborated in his *Short Organum for the* Theatre, the main aim of his "new theatre" was to provoke the audience to think about the status quo, question what is commonly accepted to be the "Truth", and to show both as alterable. In Scene 1, Ludovico

---

[1] Walder, in Brown & Gupta, p. 327
[2] in Hecht (1961), p. 54
[3] Brecht (1949)

expresses his confusion about a concave and a convex lense, one magnifying and the other one reducing, not cancelling each other out[4], an assumption that most of us would have made, too, yet we do not question how a telescope works. His use of a historical setting, moreover, emphasizes how common (and possibly wrong) beliefs have managed to survive. While scientific "ignorance" may not surprise us in a rich young man living in the 17th century, realizing that we still hold the same beliefs nowadays is disturbing and alienating. Brecht, thus, shows that some things are so obvious to us today that we take them for granted. Similarly, when Federzoni exclaims that nobody ever "checked up" on Aristotle, who had claimed that a needle could not float[5] (again, something most of us would have assumed, too), the audience is more or less explicitly invited to "check up" on old beliefs, such as the way society works. (Indirectly, the reference to Aristotle here could also be seen as a further criticism of his theatre and a justification of Brecht's new theatrical practices.)

Similar mechanisms are at work in Scene 13, inviting judgement from the spectator. Since the audience is expected to know the story of Galileo, his recantation does not need to be shown. Instead, we are presented with the expectations of his disciples and his daughter. Consequently, the spectator's interest is diverted away from the actual recantation towards its consequences, providing Brecht with the opportunity to present different perspectives. The dialectical basis is formed by the opposition of Andrea, condemning Galileo's recantation, and Galileo's justification of it. Furthermore, the Little Monk's understanding on humane grounds and the objective comment and explanation are added to the discussion. Thus, different possibilities of interpretation and judgement of the action are demonstrated and the audience is given room for reflection and their own judgement. Again, the use of history serves to reverse our expectations. Being familiar with the story of Galileo, Brecht's condemnation of his actions, even if not shared by the director's or spectator's interpretation of the play, at the very least leads the audience to question previous attitudes. Thus, independent from individual performances or theatrical effects, the text's inherent questioning of accepted "facts" and its invitation for judgement alreay embody and fulfill a large part of Brecht's aspirations.

In order to fully achieve his aims and involve the spectator's in the aforementioned process, however, Brecht thought it necessary to alienate the audience and present his argument in a dialectic manner in order to show individuals conditioned by time and class, and display "truth" as temporary and society as alterable. The two different levels of scene 13,

---

[4] p.12
[5] p.74

his disciples hoping for Galileo's resistance to the Inquisition and his daughter Virginia praying for his salvation, are, moreover, a clear example of how individuals are conditioned by their personal circumstances. While Virginia, having been religiously conditioned by the church and her father's refusal to encourage her interest in knowledge, is preoccupied with the salvation of her father's soul, Andrea acts according to his ideals and scientific beliefs. This idea of external circumstances governing human behaviour is finally fully embodied in Scene 12. Throughout the scene, the audience witnesses how the former Cardinal slowly resigns from his scientific beliefs as he is dressed and truns into Pope Urban VIII. As he hands over Galileo to the Inquisition, his robes become to symbolize the worldly, or in this case, religious circumstances that condition our behaviour. These external conditions, thus, show that human behaviour and social reality are not inherent to human nature and can, as a result, be altered, as Brecht wished to demonstrate with his "new" theatre.

However, in order to activate reason and the critical faculties that are necessary for an analysis of the issues presented to the audience, the spectator is not allowed to fall into a state of "trance", but, instead, needs to be aware of the fact that he/she is watching a *representation* of reality. Here, Brecht uses his ideas of a "historical" theatre to further his ambitions. As described by Cohen[6], history in *The Life of Galileo* is "best regarded as a "history" in something like an Elizabethan sense", Brecht having altered the original material in order to best suit his didactic purpose. The play's historical setting, *Life of Galileo* being set in the early 17th century, contributes to the embodiement of Brecht's ideas in a significant way. As stated by Antonio Regales[7] "El ser humano no es un ente intemporal que sobrevuela las diferentes epocas historicas, sino que esta historicamente condicionado y ello se refleja en la cultura y en la mentalidad"[8]. As he continues, in order to reflect upon ourselves and our world, we need to escape from the presence. Brecht used this idea in his "historical" theatre. He explains in his *Short Organum for the Theatre*[9] that the impulses which move Galileo are different due to the different historical period and that this does not only make it more difficult for the audience to identify with the main character, but also produces a greater critical attitude towards our own behaviour. Even though the play is set over 200 years before the time of its creation, there are striking similarities between the historical contexts. The Holy Inquisition and its restrictions on scientific investigation closely mirrors the effects the

---

[6] Cohen (1970) p.1
[7] Regales, p.1
[8] "The human being is not an atemporal entity that flies over different historical epochs , but instead is historically conditioned and this is reflected in culture and mentality." – my translation
[9] Brecht (1949) paragraph 37, p. 120

Third Reich and its fascist regime had on society. Thus, even though the play deals with contemporary (or atemporal) issues, such as the scientist's moral responsibility to society, they are rendered strange and unfamiliar by being set in the past, influencing our critical judgement. While "history in an Elizabethan sense" can, therefore, not be seen as something new, the use Brecht puts to it was certainly a novelty.

Even though the term "epic theatre" is mainly associated with Brecht, it also was not new, being already practised in Berlin in the 1920s by Erwin Piscator, who included films and slides in the plays he directd and produced. But while Piscator was aiming for the inclusion of the audience, Brecht used his alienation effects to exclude it. As Brecht himself admitted[10], *Galileo* is a play with "restricted" alienation effects.[11] That is not, however, to imply that they are not extensively at work. In the first production of the play in the US, Laughton beautifully embodied Brecht's theory of acting. Since the audience was not supposed to identify with the character or to fall into a "trance", the actor himself was to emphasize that he was merely *acting*, without becoming immersed in his role. Later productions, such as Losey's film version, do not achieve to fully reproduce Laughton's success, but certain features, such as Topol's direct addressing to the camera do have a similar effect. This is not to say that a Brechtian style of acting is conditioned by time, as the character of Priuli demonstrates in the film version. Cohn Blakely's body language and facial expressions, as well as his tone of voice and the pacing of his language in Scene 1, for instance, are all excellent examples of Brecht's "Gestus".

Depite the fact that Brecht's main aims are realized well in the play, some of the techniques used, especially in Losey's film version, contradict Brecht's original ideas about the theatre. One of the main techniques leading up to Aristotelian catharsis is the building up to a climax. Even though Brecht was heavily oposed to the resulting discharge of emotion and tried to avoid it through the announcement of events by means of banners or, as in the film version, a chorus, *Galileo*'s recantation scene can be seen as relatively climactic. This is especially the case in Losey's mis-en-scene in his film version, where he returns to theatrical practices in Scene 13. Throughout most of the scene both Galileo's disciples, expecting his refusal to recant, as well as Virginia, praying for his "salvation" can be seen and heard simultaneously on stage, the dramatic effect being reinforced by the huge shadows cast on the white background. The tempo is slowed down as the audience first witnesses the disciples'

---

[10] in Schumacher (1968), p.124
[11] the translation of the German *Verfremdung* does, however, only show one side of its original meaning, namely, not only to render the familiar strange, but also to make the strange appear familiar

relief when the supposed hour of Galileo's recantation has passed without the bell having been rung, creating more tension than what can be found in Brecht's earlier works and exposing the play to the "risk" of extensive emotional involvement.

As mentioned before, *Life of Galileo* does not strictly follow Brecht's theories about theatre to the same extent as do his other major plays, to a point where it still includes parts that are structured in a classical (Aristotlian) way, in particular his emphasis on symmetry. The main criticism of his play here has been that despite his personal contempt for Galileo's recantation, his protagonist still provokes empathy, chiefly through his physical passions and fears (of torture) that the audience can identify with relatively easily. Even tough Brecht had no intentions of eliminating emotions alltogether from his plays, especially Topol's lack of the Brechtian style of acting that I mentioned earlier on, lead to a rather light-hearted presentation of the protagonist that fails to represent Brecht's contempt for him.

A typically epic element, found in all of Brecht's major plays, that is present, however, are the numerous monologues that reflect and comment upon events and estrange them. Long speeches by Galileo, such as in Scene 1[12] can be found throughout the play. The estrangement of these is enhanced by abrupt changes in tone, such as Andreas remark, after Galileo's two-page long speech about the arrival of a new age, "And you'd better drink up your milk (...)"[13]. Furthermore, contradicting images are juxtaposed, such as the church's attitude and behaviour in Scene 6, wanting to profit from him at the same time as prohibiting his investigations. Similarly, many sentences are antithetically structured, presenting two opposing concepts, such as *"the old times age is over, the new age has begun"*, all cotributing to the embodiment of Brecht's ideas about alienation and dialectics within the play.

What further contributes to the alienation of the audience are the comic elements when characters contradict themselves either directly or through the divergence of their speech and their actions. The old Cardinal, in Scene 6, declares that "everything comes visibly and incontrovertibly to depend on me"[14], right before he collapses. Moreover, quotations, as part of Brecht's epic style, contribute to the alienation of the audience, especially when they transcend their original context. The religous quotations are used in a sociopolitical context, such as at Bellarmini's ball[15] (even though, ironically, the cardinals' religious quotations are not actually from the bible). The almost ridiculous nature of the "quotation duel" between

---

[12] pp.6-8
[13] p.8
[14] p. 14
[15] pp. 57-58

6

Galileo and Barberini in Scene 7, further underlined by the fact that the supposed quotation do not exist in the Bible, question, once more, the blind acceptance of "history".

The lack of some alienation effects in *Life of Galileo*, as opposed to most of his earlier plays, can certainly be attributed to the fact that by the time the play was produced in the US, Brecht had realized that his idea of an epic theatre put too great an emphasis on form in order to accurately represent and contribute to social reality. Consequently he adapted his views to a "dialectical" theatre, still maintaining the emphasis on narrative, some alienation effects but stressing, above all, its instructive aims. Brecht believed in the dialectics of the human being as the product of his environment and in his ability to change it. It was through his plays that he wanted to create an awareness of this ability and possibility to modify the very circumstances that condition human beings, the use of "historical" plays helping him to show th influences upon Galileo caused by his historical circumstances. The dialectics at work in *Life of Galileo* can, above all be seen in its aforementioned symmetrical structure. Brecht's sketch for the American version[16] clearly demonstrates this planned symmetry: Scene 1 is set in the morning, Scene 12 in the evening, a gift arrives in both scenes and a lecture is given to Andrea, just to name a few. Even though, as Schumacher[17] points out, the symmetric structure of the play is one of the features that has gained it its reputation as "conservative", Brecht uses it for his own purposes, i.e. to underline the dialectics in Galileo's life.

The dialectics in Galileo's life are furthermore reflected by the recurrent antitheses in the play. In Scene 6, Galileo's observations are confirmed by the Collegium Romanum, in the following scene, he is informed that his theories have been prohibited by the Church. As Walsh described in his review of Losey's film version[18], these are "designed to make evident the contradictory forces at work in Galileo's life, to pose positive qualities against negative, public images against private, cerebral ideas against physical passions". The result is that Galileo's character is presented in ambiguous terms, neither as positive nor as entirely negative (even though the later versions tend to suggest Brecht's own condemnation of his protagonist), once again inviting judgement.

The combination of thesis-antithesis-synthesis forms an important element in the structure of the play. Even though this can be found throughout the play, Scene 1 provides us with a particular clear example, which also introduces the main theme that is to be repeated in the following scenes. It presents us with Galileo's unrestricted belief in Science (thesis),

---

[16] quoted in Schumacher (1968), p.126
[17] Schumacher (1968), p. 126
[18] Walsh (1975)

giving a lesson to Andrea and proclaiming the arrival of a new age, only to immediately point out its limits (antithesis), with the Procurator's arrival and the manifestation of Galileo's financial needs in order to continue his research, and the potential threat of the Inquisition. The two are then synthesized in what is to foreshadow Galileo's resignation, when he instructs Andrea not to reveal their discoveries to the outside world.[19]

While Losey's film version of the play does stay very close to the original's structural alienation effects, this very fact poses a problem in relation to contemporary expectations. Its episodic structure, the chorus announcing events or commenting on action, printed titles or, in the case of theatre performances, banners and writing on curtains were intended to be something strange and unfamiliar. However, as Walsh[20] states, "in the intervening twenty-eight years audiences have become so used to such devices that they no longer function efficaciously." In part, this is due to the differences in teatre and film. While Brecht had used banners announcing what the audience is about to see, the film uses subtitles, an accepted technique often used to *maintain* the illusion of verisimilitude, not to eliminate it, such as is the case in the wide range of crime investigation series on television. Consequently, we do no longer perceive them as "disturbing", which would lead us to think critically, but are, instead, more likely to follow the action passively. As I mentioned earlier on, Brecht was conscious of the need to adapt these kind of effects. Losey, as well as most directors, however, merely copied Brecht's old devices instead of recreating the desired effect.

In conclusion, it is understandable why some critics may have come to regard the play as conservative and not in line with Brecht's dramatic theory. Nevertheless, even though his use of history and symmetric structure, combined with the lack of alienation effects, when compared to his other major plays, seem to indicate that *Life of* Galileo was a step backwards, his overall aims are still fulfilled, at least as far as his original version is concerned. Conflicts with Brecht's ideas have, however, arisen in subsequent performances due to the fact that directors merely copied Brecht's "old" devices instead of reproducing their effect. This failure in reproducing Brecht's alienation effects significantly reduced the play's original intentions. Having said this, however, the play does continuously question our acceptance of the "truth" and social reality and does inherently encourage the audience to see its power to change it. . Despite the fact that some of his "new" effects have ceased to be new, his use of history, which remains and always will remain history, ensures that emotional involvement is restricted and the audience is invited to question commonly held beliefs, all at the same time

---

[19] p.18
[20] Walsh, 1975

as being entertained. I think we have been able to see that *Life of Galileo*, at least in its last version and directed by Brecht in the play's early years of performance, did indeed embody his ideas of a new theatre.

References

Blau, H. (). *The Thin, Thin Crust and the Colophon of Doubt: The Audience in Brecht.* New Literary History, Vol. 21, No. 1, (Autumn, 1989), pp.175-197

Brecht, B. (1949). *A Short Organum for the Theatre.* in Eagleton, T. & Milne, D. (eds) (1996). *Marxist Literary Theory: A Reader.* Oxford: Blackwell Publishing

Brecht, B. (1986). *Life of Galileo.* London: Methuen

Brown, R.D. & Gupta, S. (eds) (2005). *Aestheticism & Modernism: Debating Twentieth-Century Literature 1900-1960.* London:Routledge in association with The Open University

Cohen, M.A. (1970). *History and Moral in Brecht's "Life of Galileo".* Contemporary Literature, Vol. 11, No. 1 (Winter, 1970), pp. 80-97

Curran, A. (2001). *Brecht's Criticism of Aristotle's Aesthetics of Tragedy.* The Journal of Aesthetics and Art Criticism, Vol. 59, No.2, (Spring, 2001), pp.167-184

Fehervary, H. (1976). *Enlightenment or Entanglement: History and Aesthetics in Bertolt Brecht and Heiner Müller.* New German Critique, No. 8, (Spring, 1976), pp.80-109

Freeman, M. (1999). *Truth and Justice in Bertolt Brecht.* Cardozo Studies in Law and Literature, Vol. 11, No.2, (Winter, 1999), pp. 197-214

Fuegi, J. (1974). *Toward a Theory of Dramatic Literature for a Technological Age.* Educational Theatre Journal, Vol. 26, No. 4, (Dec., 1974), pp. 433-440

Gassner, J. (1955). *Forms of Modern Drama.* Comparative Literature, Vol. 7, No. 2, Changing Perspectives in Modern Literature: A Symposium, (Spring, 1955), pp.129-143

Goodman, H. (1952). *Bertolt Brecht as "Traditional" Dramatist.* Educational Theatre Journal, Vol, 4, No. 2, (May, 1952), pp. 109-114

Gupta, S.& Johnson, D. (eds) (2005). *A Twentieth-Century Literature Reader.* London:Routledge in association with The Open University

Hecht, W. (1961). *The Development of Brecht's Theory of the Epic Theatre 1918-1933.* The Tulane Drama Review, Vol. 6, No. 1, (Sep., 1961), pp. 40-97

Longree,G.H.F. (1966). *Epic Theater:A Marxist and a Catholic Interpretation.* The South Central Bulletin, Vol. 26, No. 4, Studies by Members of SCMLA, (Winter, 1966), pp.51-57

Lunn, E. (1974). *Marxism and Art in the Era of Stalin and Hitler:A Comparison of Brecht and Lukacs.* New German Critique, No. 3, (Autumn, 1974), pp.12-44

Moore, A. (2002). *Studying Bertolt Brecht.* available at http://www.universalteacher.org.uk/drama/brecht.htm. (accessed 02/06/07)

Regales, A. *La mentalidad actual y la mentalidad medieval a la luz de la literatura.* Universidad de Valladoid

Reinelt, J. (1985). *Bertolt Brecht and Howard Brenton: The Comon Task.* Pacific Coast Philolgy, Vol. 20, No. 1/2, (Nov., 1985), pp.46-52

Schumacher, E. & Neugroschel, J. (1968). *The Dialectics of "Galileo".* TDR (1967-1968), Vol. 12, No. 2. (Winter 1968). pp. 124-133

Sohlich, W. (1993). *The Dialectics of Mimesis and Rperesentation in Brecht's "Life of Galileo".* Theater Journal Vol. 45, No. 1. German Theatre after the F/Wall. (Mar.1993), pp. 49-64

Steer, W.A.J. (1968). *Brecht's Epic Theater: Theory and Practice.* The Modern Language Review, Vol. 63, No. 3, (Jul., 1968), pp. 636-649

Suvin, D. (1976). *The Mirror and the Dynamo.* TDR (1967-1968), Vol. 12, No. 1 (Autumn 1967). pp. 56-67

Walsh, M. (1975). *Galileo: Losey , Brecht and Galileo.* Jump Cut, no. 7, 1975, pp. 13-15. available at http://www.ejumpcut.org/archive/onlinessays/JC07folder/galileo.html (accessed 25/05/07)

Weber, C (1980). *Brecht in Eclipse?.* The Drama Review: TDR, Vol. 24, No. 1, German Theatre Issue. (Mar., 1980), pp.115-124

Weber, C & Munk, E. (1976). *Brecht as Director.* TDR (1967-1968), Vol. 12, No. 1 (Autumn 1967). pp. 101-107

YOUR KNOWLEDGE HAS VALUE

- We will publish your bachelor's and master's thesis, essays and papers

- Your own eBook and book - sold worldwide in all relevant shops

- Earn money with each sale

Upload your text at www.GRIN.com
and publish for free